# Advance Praise for Dr. Claudia Barnett and The Dissertation Process...

"*The Dissertation Process: A Step-by-Step Mentored Guide* is a must-have for those pursuing a PhD. There is so much valuable and insightful information included in this practical guide! Dr. Barnett has covered several aspects of the Dissertation process that has *not* been discussed. This resource will do your doctoral journey good!"
— **Kim M. Campbell, Doctoral Candidate**

"In writing this book, Dr. Barnett has performed an invaluable service. Many survivors of the doctoral journey have written on the process of writing a dissertation. However, Dr. Barnett has also filled the void of information on the psychological and emotional toil necessary to succeed at the highest level of academic study. As she so astutely addresses, earning a doctoral degree requires as much tenacity as intellect. Success depends on knowing how to handle the vicissitudes of the doctoral journey. This book is a "must read" for everyone who is contemplating pursuing a doctoral degree or is already engaged in the process."
— **Pearl Richardson Smith, Ph.D., President Pearl of Wisdom Solutions**

"*The Dissertation Process: A Step-by-Step Mentored Guide* speaks to the emotional and scholastic experiences that have been either overlooked or temporarily forgotten. Because this process is unique in nature, it is difficult at times to have someone to share similar thoughts with. Dr. Barnett addresses the changes as well as challenges that one will encounter, along with providing insight from a mentored perspective. This is a must read for those who enjoy the practical application of knowledge and experience that is conveyed by those who are involved in a mentoring relationship. It is a resourceful tool..."
— **Marcia Brandon, Ph.D. Co-Founder/Regional Director, Caribbean Group of Youth Business Trusts**

"Without using the exact words, Dr. Barnett has essentially defined a dissertation as a kind of psychological warfare. She peels back the layers and reveals what no one else has so clearly and precisely defined. She takes the reader inside the characteristic mental struggle that occurs when completing a dissertation and gives comprehensive tools to mitigate this struggle. Dr. Barnett's book is a must-have tool for anyone who wants to understand the psychological warfare that occurs during the dissertation-writing. The reader will learn how to win the psychological war and be one of the few who complete the process. *Any* individual completing a dissertation should *read this book first.*"

—**Carlos Todd, Ph.D., LPC, NCC, CAMF**
**President, Conflict Coaching & Consulting, LLC**

"Dr .Barnett has touched on the integral parts of the dissertation process. Although your institution sets the required standards, Dr. Barnett expresses the practical blend of emotional and the scholastic process that one will go through. From the perspective of those *who are in a Masters' degree* program seeking information about the process, to those who are actively pursuing the Doctoral degree, Dr. Barnett brings a level of "practicality" that is shared as a mentor. For those who want to springboard into this process with clarity, I would suggest reviewing this book."

—**Jamie Barron, Ed.D.**
**Capella University**
**Chair, Training & Performance Improvement PhD, MS**
**Chair, Educational Leadership and Management Ed.D.**

"This step-by-step mentoring guide, *The Dissertation Process*, written by Dr. Barnett, is in my opinion, the best investment that you can make to be successful on your doctoral journey. Dr. Barnett remembers her doctoral journey--her struggles and encourages *you* to stay focused. If you earnestly follow her plan of action, you will become a doctor. This book is not only a guide for the doctoral process; it is a guide for successful living."

—**Dr. Mary White Williams**
**Retired Educator and Pastor**

"*The Dissertation Process: A Step-by-Step Mentoring Guide* is truly a wonderful book as I found it to be very interesting. It is unique as it delivers the practical level of the approach to the dissertation process, which is valuable. A great and informative read, I would highly recommend this extraordinary book as a must have for anyone interested in pursuing their Ph.D."

— **Venkat Edara, MBA, Ph.D.**
**Chief Technical Officer, ITS Inc.**
**Adjunct Professor, Chancellor University**


"*The Dissertation Process: A Step-by-Step Mentored Guide* is a must read for every doctoral candidate! Dr. Barnett lays out the process in a way that is easy to follow. Her method of responding to frequently asked questions provides the Doctoral learner with a resource of relevant answers. With the array of emotions that arise, this book makes it virtually impossible for candidates to fail or stop at the "All but Dissertation" (ABD) level. By exercising Dr. Barnett's mentoring techniques through the entire process, the reader with gain all the benefits of increased knowledge. If you know someone who is involved in a Masters program and has an interest in pursuing their Doctorate, this book will provide a wonderful guide through their anticipated journey. I highly recommend this book."

— **Dr. Patricia W. Brumfield, Independent Corporate Trainer**


"This mentored guide to the dissertation process was exactly what I needed as a doctoral learner. The content was easy to follow and digest amidst the monumental amounts of reading and research required of a PhD candidate. This guide was different; it wasn't a "how to" guide or a "get a PhD fast with no effort" book. Dr. Barnett was very honest about the journey, and in many cases, offered answers and opportunities to reflect on questions that may not have been asked yet. I highly recommend this guide as a resource to supplement the information you will receive from your institution of higher learning."

— **Kenisha L. Thompson, M.Ed, PhD Candidate**
**President, Keni Consulting, LLC**

"Finally! A purposely written, comprehensive, nuts and bolts guide. This resource provides doctoral candidates with a step-by-step roadmap through the often daunting dissertation process. This easy to read guide removes the fear that materializes, and enables as well as encourages one to conquer the dissertation process. Unfortunately, this book was not around when I was walking through the experience..."

— **Dr. M.B. Haughton, Organizational Developer**

"Dr. Barnett has removed all doubts in accomplishing one's dissertation in the Ph.D. process, by answering the emotional questions that will arise as well as the practical questions in achieving the highest level of education desired for one's self. The encouragement through mentoring from this book is bound to increase the number of Ph.D.'s in our country and the world. I am so proud to have Dr. Barnett as a friend, sister, and mentor in my life for over 20 years."

— **Alextrae Stokes-McClendon-MPA**
**Compass- Life Coach**

"Dr. Barnett and I have shared the dissertation journey and beyond. She practices what she preaches. Her emphasis on your personal and academic journey is relevant and valuable. Important characteristics such as academic preparation and resources are vital. The incorporation of personal resources including: time management, support networks, and self-assessment are relevant. Dr. Barnett addresses each of these topics with wisdom and compassion. It is of the utmost importance to take her advice to heart. Overall, it will make your dissertation journey more manageable and meaningful."

— **Pamela L. Robinson, Ph.D., Faculty Capella University**

"If you are considering pursuing a PhD program or you are working on your dissertation, *The Dissertation Process: A Step-by-Step Mentored Guide* is a must have! Dr. Barnett provides a detailed mentoring experience that dissertation practitioners are in *need* of, while on the scholarly road. This guide is spot on!"

— **Saudia Muhammad, Ph.D.**
**Educator, DeKalb County School District**

# The Dissertation Process
## A Step-by-Step Mentored Guide

Claudia G. Barnett, Ph.D.

Copyright © 2011 by Claudia G. Barnett, Ph.D.
Second Printing

All rights reserved. No portion of this book may be reproduced — mechanically, electronically, or by any other means, including photocopying — without written permission of the author.

ISBN: 978-1479294947

Cover illustrations by R'Tish Creations

The Dissertataion Process books are available at special discounts when purchased in bulk for premiums and sales promotions as well as fundraising or educational use.

Contact: info@thedissertationprocess.com for further information or instruction.

Printed in the United States of America

## Dedication

To those who aspire to be a PhD;
Philosophiae Doctor (Doctor of Philosophy) and
a scholar practitioner; may your *desires*
become the reality.

# Contents

Forward
Preface

Chapter 1
**Am I Really Doing This? (Analysis)** ...............1
What The? (The Series of Questions) • I Thought I Went Through Some Rigor in My Course Work • I Knew the Process Was Intense, But I Had No Idea • Yes, I Am DOING This!

Chapter 2
**What Have I Gotten Myself Into? (Self Assessment)** .......................................................11
Although I Did the Course Work • Am I Really Smart Enough? • Have I Counted All of the Costs? • The Reality Check

Chapter 3
**No Turning Back; I've Got Too Much Invested (Consequences)** ............................17
I Spent a Lot of Time and Money • What Are My Possible Options? • Do I Know What I Am Thinking — Really? • Weighing All of the Variables

Chapter 4
**Are You Serious? ( The Reality Check)** ..... 25
Phases and Levels of Seriousness • Now That I Know Where I Am • Plan of Action • Follow-Up and Follow Through

Chapter 5
**I Can Research, I Can Write – Can't I? (Doubt)** ............... 33
Second Guessing Yourself • Where Did You Get That Idea? • How to Do I Select a Topic? • Skill Level, Skill Set • Accepting the Challenge of Being Challenged

Chapter 6
**I'm Half –Way Through (Anticipation)** ... 43
Confronting or Conforming – Which Is It? • Loving My Work • Ways of Improving Because of New Findings • Inclusion vs. Exclusion

Chapter 7
**The Detours (Psychological Challenges)** .. 49
Life Happens • React or Respond • You Have Choices – Do You Make One? • Re-evaluation of Everything – Sticking to Your Decision

Chapter 8
**Getting On Course Again (Educational and Self Assessment)** .............................. 53
The Epiphany • Re-evaluating How to Regain Lost Time • Making Comparisons to the Other Similarities In Your Life • Coming Back With a Vengeance

Chapter 9
**Smoother Sailing (Confidence)** .................. 57
Some Not Always Approved • Re-evaluate the Subject Matter • The Back and Forth Dance

Chapter 10
**Is the End Really in Sight? (Expectation)** ... 63
Formulating Plans for Life After the Process • Getting Involved With Outside Professional Sources and Resources

Chapter 11
**The Process CAN Become a Reality (Achievement)** .................................................. 65
The Defense • The Necessary Details • Final Preparations • Getting Approved After the Approval • Gearing Up for the Ceremony/Celebration

Chapter 12
**Closing Out This and Other Chapters in Your Life (Re-evaluation)** ..................................... 75
Taking a Bird's Eye View of This Process • Reuniting With Family and Loved Ones • Assessing Relationships • Understanding Values: Mentally, Socially, Psychologically, Spiritually

Chapter 13
**True Self-Assessment (Reality)** .................. 83
Understanding the Magnitude • Embracing the Process

Chapter 14
**Loving Me and Proud of It (Professional Assessment)** ...................................................... 85
Re-evaluation of the Work Completed — Registering With the Authorities (Validation) • Understanding the Total Me

Chapter 15
**Let Me Share What I Have Done! (Pride and Satisfaction)** ...................................................... 89
My Contribution to the Body of Knowledge • Plans From This Point On — Assessment on a Regular Basis How Do I Keep the Passion Going? • Giving Back

Closing Thoughts ................................................. 93

**BONUS:**
Appendix A: The Foundational Components of a Dissertation ..................... 99
Appendix B: Preparing for the Institutional Review Board (IRB) ..................... 107

# Forward

If you are looking for a guide to assist you through the dissertation process that is "step-by-step" and written by a person who has been through the trenches and successfully out to the other side, this is the book for you. I have sat on over fifty dissertation committees over the past 10 to 15 years. I was Dr. Barnett's mentor through her dissertation process and I feel I am the best person to understand her learning process, as well as her struggles. I also witnessed her excitement on the day of her final journey when she received the elusive acronym of Ph.D. I also experienced her excitement and passion to share her practical experience with others who were awaiting the same journey.

Dr. Barnett's book exhibits various tools to assist you "step-by-step" as the title states. She provides excellent advice on how to tackle not only the actual technical requirements of the dissertation process, but also the psychological challenges of the process that all doctoral students must experience to be successful. The guideposts on the cover of this book identify the feelings and frustrations that all doctoral students must address to complete a doctoral process. By linking the positive and negative issues that she encountered, along with this step-by-step guide, Dr. Barnett offers numerous words of wisdom that will assist you on an academic and on a personal level.

I always remind my mentees while they travel through their dissertation process, the journey is tough but the destination is worth it. Knowing this information, you have to plan it, live it, do it, and be patient. Dr. Barnett has put these challenges into words and has broken them down into phases, so that anyone that wishes to embark on a doctoral journey can use this guide to assist them from beginning to end. The doctoral process is an *individual and isolated* journey. The doctoral candidates that *use the "step-by-step" process* identified in this guide will realize that they are really not alone.

I congratulate Dr. Claudia Barnett for taking the time to write and share her experiences and recommendations with everyone, to assist them in the doctoral process. She truly is a mentor, as her guide is all about assisting you to live your dream. Enjoy the book and good luck on your doctoral journey.

Dr. Mike
Michael H. McGivern, Ph. D.
Organizational Development Consultant, Adjunct Professor
Conference Presenter & Researcher

# Preface

The journey of becoming a doctor, a PhD in particular, is life-changing—you actually become a different individual in the process. Working through the coursework, and acquiring knowledge along the way is just a small part of the process. The PhD is the highest level of formal education that one can achieve, and the individuals who actually achieve this designation go through some "psychological war wounds" in the process. However, this aspect is *not* usually discussed. Why? Generally, because most individuals are so mentally "whipped" by the time they complete this process and they are so elated to be finished they only want to put the experience behind them. But that does not help those who come after them to understand the process, so this is a tell-all book because I believe you should know what you are getting into from the start.

I know you probably already have some hesitations or reservations about starting the PhD process as well as some pointed questions. Why am I doing this, really? Am I sure that I want to do this? What or to whom am I trying to prove something? The reality of it is that to succeed *you* have to want this really, really badly. You cannot be fueled by the notion that this desire alone (if not genuine) will keep you motivated. My real purpose in writing this book is to explain the various phases that one *will and must* go through in order to achieve this rigorous degree. It is by no means for the faint of heart as you will see as you read this book. It is a degree obtained through persistence. Do you have what it takes to keep you going? My role as a doctoral mentor is to assist you with the practical methods of the process, in addition to sharing the possible psychological challenges that you will face. Overall, if you believe in yourself, and consult your higher authority, you too will be successful and achieve all that is to be a part of your life plan.

Blessings,
Dr. Claudia

Chapter 1

# Am I Really Doing This? (Analysis)

This is a really big move. You've made the decision to go to school and; pursue an advanced degree, and now you are at a crossroad. You have to keep asking yourself; "Am I really doing this?" Well, for now, the answer is "yes." However, you did not just happen here. Getting here is the result of conscious thought and consideration. Over time, you consistently made decisions that allowed you to get you to this point.

Let's go back and look at how you got here. In general, people do what they desire to do. Your current status or station in life is the result of past decisions and achievements that include a host pressures and expectations from your peers and families that you may have chosen to adapt or ignore. When you examine this area closer, you can reflect on topics like "human motivation." This encompasses the important distinction between whether behavior is autonomous or controlled.

*Autonomy.* People often equate autonomy to being in accordance with one's self—feeling a sense of freedom without restrictions, like having the ability and power to use one's will. A characteristic of this behavior is the ability to be truly interested along with being committed to the activity. In contrast, one who is controlled is involved as a result of being pressured. When controlled individuals act without a sense of personal endorsement, their behavior is not an extension or expression of themselves because it has been strongly influenced by a control mechanism. We have all experienced this type of personal influence and to some extent it is always present in our lives.

Let's look at how people are influenced by the factors of human motivation. Figure 1 illustrates this process. Your approach to the process will have a tremendous impact on your performance as well as morale.

In figure 1, we see that autonomy produces freedom, and authenticity (to self) is a by-product. Integration or the psychological process of understanding autonomy along with authenticity can also be a defining aspect of self as well. However, it is there only in a supportive role. On the controlled side, there are some restrictions. *Controlled* has the two factors of influence: compliance and defiance. These two variables form an unstable partnership that can go either way.

Figure 1  Understanding the dynamics of Human Motivation

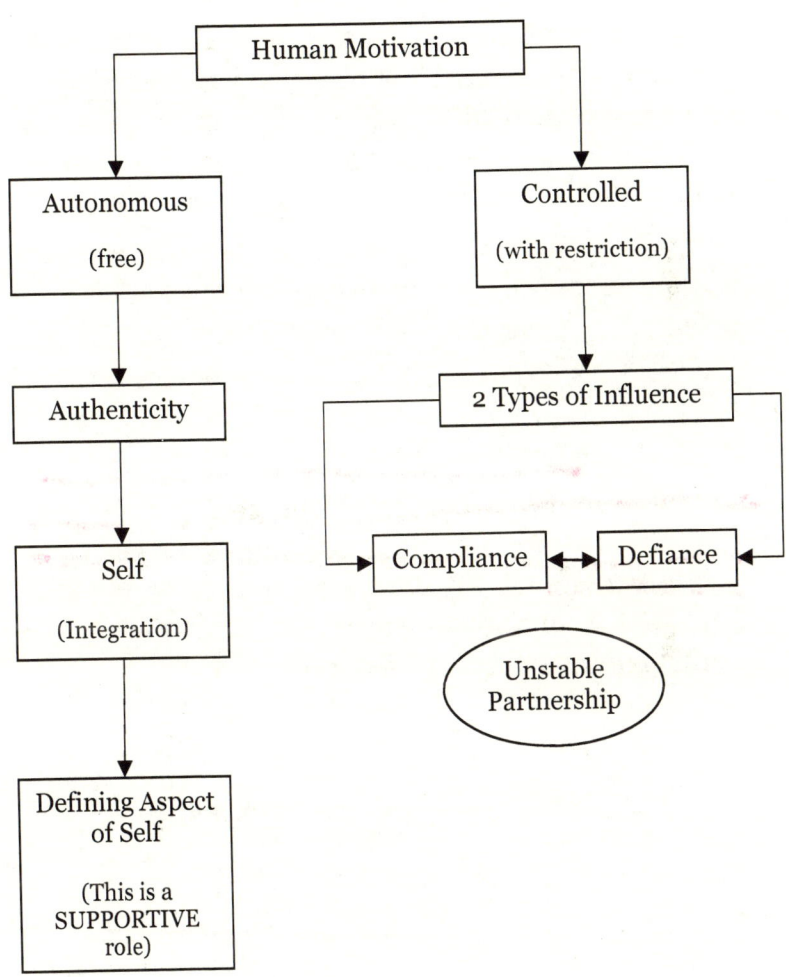

Acting autonomously creates authenticity. This action promotes being true to one's inner self and is a catalyst for success. As we review the reasons why people do what they do, (in this case pursuing an advanced degree and writing this final research project) you must have a full understanding of why you are embarking on this process. You need to go into it for the correct reasons. Ultimately, your approach to this process will have a tremendous impact on your performance as well as your overall morale. Additional research by psychologist Edward Deci supports this theory. Deci believed that once a person's sense of autonomy is supported success *will* occur. In other words, the combination of a task that is important to you and the allowance of as much personal freedom as possible to carry it out will stimulate interest and commitment making this process a more effective approach than the standard system of reward and punishment.

## What The? (The Series of Questions)

As you review your recent accomplishments, you may have a sense of pride and achievement. You have fulfilled the required examinations, assessments, writing, etc. All of these requirements have somewhat validated your status. You are well on your way to achieve that desired degree. Now you are becoming aware of bits and pieces of information — vital information that is coming at you from several directions. It all has to do with how you will approach this final project.

*Yes*, this is a project. You will be working at this topic for an extended amount of time. Depending on your previous training, this may easily be the most dedicated time that you will have spent on anything on a continuous basis, including report writing for your current profession. You will have information from your educational institution, seminars, and suggestions from your colleagues, plus your own findings from your proposed research topic. Looking at it all, you take a breath and almost desire to use a few choice words, primarily due to the constant influx of information coming your way. Making a statement of *"What the...?"* is a simple way of questioning the present moment, while you catch your breath. As you fill out the rest of the sentence, you may even end up with just one word posed as a question: "What?" The word "what" can be phrased: "What are they (the school) expecting of me? What are the requirements again? What is the required time period that I have to work within? What are the resources available to assist me in this process?" As you answer these questions and many others like them that will come your way, you will begin to structure a plan of action.

It is important that you take the next step which is to fill in the gaps to develop a more detailed action plan that can lead you to success. Ironically, as you complete this step, this will also be the time when you may question yourself and your ability. This too is normal. Although this behavior may not have been discussed by your peers (who are now PhD's,) they too had their "what the?" moments. This type of reaction is to be expected in response to the various levels of information that will come your way. You've heard the adage: *"your attitude determines your altitude."* Well you have some important choices to make. In order to be successful, you must be true to yourself and to your level of commitment. The next question is, "How badly do you really want this?"

## I Thought I Went Through Some Rigor in My Course Work...

During this transitional time, you start to reflect on days gone by. Do you remember when you started your first class? Can you remember being presented with the syllabus and the requirements for your course? How did you feel then? Were you calm or were you overwhelmed in thought and questioning your ability to accomplish it all?

These questions and countless others like them became a part of the pre-requisites as you started your

## Am I Really Doing This?

doctoral journey. Expectations were high, yet unclear. You knew that you were going to go through more detailed work and possible research as a result of your commitment. You delved into the coursework, and with the completion of each course, you continued to build the strong, solid foundation on which you are standing now. Professors wanted you to "clarify" your thought processes as you defended your point of view. Classmates challenged your statements and viewpoints although they themselves were not familiar with what you were trying to achieve. As a result of all of this, you became more knowledgeable about your subject matter and more confident in your responses. All of this assisted you in the educational process. You were challenged both from an emotional and a psychological perspective, yet you remained hopeful. You realized that if you could just translate the requirements into bite-sized tasks you would be able to not only pace yourself, but possibly apply yourself to this commitment.

Now that you are taking reflective glances back at your coursework achievements, you remember it was rigorous, yet attainable. However, as you look forward to the dissertation process, it can seem overwhelming. After all, it will most likely be the biggest research project you will ever encounter. So you ask: Can I do this next phase? Can I achieve all that is asked and expected of me? In the end, the answer is yes; primarily because you realize that you will be able to review the expectations beforehand and satisfy deadlines as you have in the past. Once you review the requirements, you will see that this project is attainable. From past experience, you already know that the easiest way to approach a task of this magnitude is to break it down into smaller projects. This will allow you to stay focused and on task to produce optimum achievement.

## I Knew the Process Was Intense, But I Had No Idea...

You have probably heard stories from those who have achieved a PhD. They most likely mentioned the intensity and rigorousness of the process. They possibly even talked about committee members and their requirements, deadlines and the personalities of some of the associated characters; among other things. But still going into this, most individuals have no idea or reference point about this process. After all, you have never been down this road before, so it's difficult to predict what to expect. And to complicate matters even more, the journey is different for every person, so there is no real blueprint to follow. What is important is that you stay focused and keep your eyes on the desired result—obtaining your PhD. You have worked in environments before where you had to be strong and persevere. This is the same posture you must take now. *Fortitude* is the word that will keep you going. It is important that you develop a mindset that keeps you focused on the end result and the impact it can have on your life once you have your degree. This is your big incentive to keep the process moving forward.

## Yes, I Am DOING This!

After careful reflection, you have made the decision to proceed. YES, you are going to do this! You have had the private conversations with yourself in the shower, in the bathroom mirror, and your other favorite places. You have weighed the pros, the cons, the good, the bad, and you have had countless arguments with yourself about why you should or should *not* continue. However, it keeps coming back to this. At this point, you have already invested at least one and a half to two years of your time and energy with coursework. If you stop now, you will miss out on any reward for your hard work, so deciding to continue is the most logical conclusion. From this point on, anyone who asks you how you are doing provides you with the opportunity to reconfirm how serious you are about this commitment. The continuous questioning about your status helps you become more resolved in your decision. *It is as though you are being held accountable through constant status updates.* Although others may not realize the seriousness and intensity of the questions posed, *you* do. This accountability check is a piece of what you need to stay in the game. Going back and forth with your decision is to be expected, and it is normal. It is just another part of the transitional phase on your doctoral journey. I am truly glad that you have decided to be proactive and continue the journey.

Chapter 2

# What Have I Gotten Myself Into? (Self-Assessment)

At times, we ask ourselves the same questions over and over again, always anticipating different answers. Although that is being unrealistic, we still tend to do this on a regular basis.

Self-concept, also known as self-identity, is almost synonymous with self-assessment. This construct (which is multi-dimensional) has several characteristics, including gender roles, sexuality, and racial identity along with academics and non-academics. Research in this area shows that individuals have an understanding of themselves by the age of three and that parents, peers, and teachers continuously reinforce this impression. These concepts of how we view ourselves involve cognitive as well as emotional impressions that produce feelings such as happiness, self-esteem, satisfaction, and anxiety along with social integration.

Psychologists Carl Rogers and Abraham Maslow established the concept of self-assessment and self-actualization. Rogers identified the significance of striving to become more like an "ideal self." He believed that the closer one is to "their ideal self" the happier he or she will be. Likewise, the term "academic self-concept" (ASC) outlined by Trautwein, Ludtke, Nagy, and Marsh in 2009 refers to this same concept of striving to become one's ideal self on the academic side.[1]

Maslow's perspective on self-assessment or his "hierarchy of needs" is shown in figure 2 on the next page. His model indicates that basic, low-level needs, such as physiological requirements and safety are areas that must be satisfied before higher-level needs such as self-fulfillment are pursued. As the diagram shows, when a need is satisfied, it is no longer a source of motivation and the next higher need takes its place. Self-actualization forms the apex of Maslow's motivation theory. Self-actualization is the quest to reach one's full potential as a person. However, this concept can be somewhat illusive. Unlike lower level needs, this need is never completely satisfied. From another perspective, as you grow psychologically, there are always new opportunities to continue to grow.

Figure 2  Maslow's hierarchy of needs

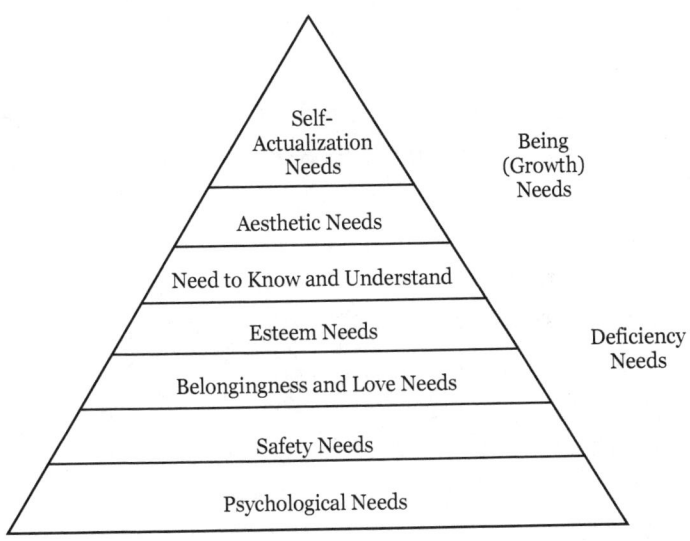

## Although I Did the Course Work...

Conducting a personal assessment can help you clarify your position. As you start to categorize and analyze all that you have done so far, such as the different courses you have taken, you will have an opportunity to look for connections and links to their relevance to your subject matter as well as your profession. Tying the relevance of what you have learned thus far with the potential of what you will learn (as a result of your upcoming doctoral research) is a key component. As you go through this stage, you may get to the point where you question your ability. Remember, you are able to complete this process, and more importantly, you will. It is critical is that you understand that the coursework you have completed is a major part of the overall process. While it is not a full indicator of what will be reflected in your research, it will provide a wonderful academic foundation on which you can build. The questions that you have in reference to completing this doctoral process are normal at this point. You will do well, and you will have much success as a result of the rigor that you have endured during the coursework phase.

## Am I Really Smart Enough?

Yes, you are smart enough. Although you have been faced with a multitude of challenges, the doctoral process is primarily one of determination and consistency. It is not a degree of intelligence specifically, but more of endurance. Having the ability to challenge yourself and to be challenged by others is a part of the process, and you will have to be on top of your game, so to speak, at all times. You will not be able to "get by" with mediocre activity. You will have to be accountable to yourself as well as others, specifically those on your doctoral committee. The word "smart" will now take on a different meaning. Beyond intelligence, it will also mean that you are consciously accountable for all of your related doctoral actions.

## Have I Counted All of the Costs?

So many variables have to be considered. By this time, you have experienced some costs, like sacrificing your time and money. Going into this, you knew there would be a financial commitment that would grow as you continued to enroll in additional courses. Still you continued on your journey. And, there are also significant time costs or commitments. It's not unusual for families to start to complain at some point that you are spending too much time on your "so-called school work." They may not understand that there is a tremendous difference between being involved in a course and the transitional stage of being "independent" in your new status of becoming a "researcher." With that said your time management skills will now be put to a rigorous test. You will have to be able to determine what is important now and what can be addressed later. Throughout your doctoral journey, things will keep coming up, and you will have to make priority decisions as each one arises.

## The Reality Check

Now, the reality sets in. You have decided to complete this monumental task. So what do you do next? You have committed to the completion of your dissertation. Whatever it takes—the sacrifice of sleep, time, social events, and other important events that will come up as you go through this process. The question is: "Are you *okay* with that?" The reality is that you will miss some (a lot) of these events, and you must be okay with that because right now it is important that you stay focused on the end result—becoming a PhD. Having the mindset that you are "all about business" will help you be successful as time passes.

Chapter 3

# No Turning Back; I've Got Too Much Invested (Consequences)

## I've spent a Lot of Time and Money

As you reflect on what you have achieved thus far, you know there is still more to come. Of course anything worth having will require the dedication of time, energy, resources and commitment. Not only have you made the decision to become a scholar-practitioner, but you have also made the commitment to contribute to a body of knowledge. When you keep the result in mind, you should be rejuvenated with the idea of the prize. During the coursework period, you have made an investment in yourself and in your future—from the purchasing of the textbooks to researching various supportive articles and documents. In the process, you created a foundational knowledge base that you can refer to not only now, but in the future as well. Regardless of the path you choose, your investment will have long-lasting benefits.

Although you have an understanding that this venture will be a significant financial investment, you may not have considered how much you will need to spend beyond tuition and books. This is primarily because you have no point of reference. As you advance in the process, different items will require an immediate financial investment. Some examples include:

- Costs to purchase of specific software packages like SPSS and NVivo
- Costs to use test instruments and surveys
- Costs associated with using research assistants
- Professional copy editing services
- Printing and binding costs
- Postage

In some instances, these are things you might like or that would make the process easier, however in others they are required, and the costs can quickly add up. As you get further involved in the dissertation process, the scope of your research will also become a determining factor in how much you will need to spend. For example, if your research is *quantitative* based (statistical in nature) you may need to consider the use of test instruments and computer software programs like SPSS. While some services such as online survey tools allow limited free subscriptions, in general, you will not be able to use the trial version of anything because of your extended time frame. If on the other hand your research is *qualitative* (involving live human subjects), you will need to allow extra time and money for facilities and scheduling complexities when working with human subjects. In time, you will learn that the time frame you may have estimated does not always coordinate with the realities of life. Things happen, and it is in your best interest to accept them as a part of the journey.

## What Are My Possible Options?

There will be times when you will question your decision to continue with the doctoral process. The question that tends to arises most often is: "If I don't do this, what are my possible options?" And you can't ignore this. You must consider the pros and the cons of your decision. Although you have already invested years in this process, you must consider both sides of this scenario. If necessary, do this exercise:

Get a sheet of paper out and divide it down the middle vertically. On one side, label on the top of the sheet the word "PROS'" and on the other side label "CONS." Ask yourself this question in the upper middle portion of the paper: *"What are the advantages and disadvantages of completing this doctoral degree?"* As you think about the possible answers, a sense of clarification should be revealed regarding whether or not to continue or discontinue the process. It is important to be truthful in your response to accept and enforce your decision.

If you decide to stay, as time progresses, you may come up with some additional responses as to why you should continue; however, the real key is being self-fulfilled. This will allow you to stay on track and work toward the completion of your task.

## Do I Know What I Am Thinking — Really?

There are times when you may second-guess yourself quite a bit. You get excited about your ideas, but when it comes time to implementing them, you may back down. You loose our enthusiasm and stamina. What are you really thinking? How are you going to map out a strategy if you are not sure of the course of action? When this occurs, it is critical to get an understanding, a clear perception of what you want. You have to have the big picture in mind, the goal, and your desired results. If we take the time to give this some thought, we may come up with some favorable answers. The question is: "Are my thoughts clear enough to follow and execute?" If they aren't, you must get to a point where you can achieve that.

## Weighing All of the Variables

Now that you have completed a few elements of the doctoral process—the coursework, and possibly your standardized exam or writing criteria—you are now ready for the next phase. In this next phase, the writing of the dissertation, fantasy meets reality.

Typically, when you get to this phase you are imagining the "completed" work—this is the fantasy illusion. The reality is so much more complicated, and in writing your dissertation several areas of your life will be impacted. For better or for worse, your new commitment to your project will impact your personal, family, work, career, finances, health, and your psychological outlook. You will not only be concerned about your scholastic status, but also your perceptions (along with relationships) and the dedication of time. The question is, "Are you really prepared for all this?"

Often the thought process is to "jump" into the writing of the dissertation and to "knock it out" in a year or even a few months. In determining whether this is a realistic time frame, you must keep in mind all that is required to achieve your desired result. To achieve optimum success, there are many areas to be considered as well as the inevitable steps in the process that require time that are often beyond your control. Let's examine a few of the areas that will be impacted, but are rarely discussed.

First is the enormous amount of time that is needed to produce an "outstanding" project. At this point in time, it may be a good idea to contact your institution to go over their requirements with as much detail as possible. Your goal is to make sure you have a clear understanding of what is required before you really start the process. As you reflect on your research study topic, some specifics to consider include: How am I going to arrive at my desired destination in this research process? Will I prove my hypothesis using quantitative or qualitative methods? Which area of research intrigues me the most? Am I going to be able to be passionate about my research area a year from now? Two years from now? Can I devote countless hours in writing and investigating supportive information and still find ways to keep this research new and appealing?

Some additional areas to consider include the following:

- The cost of this education based on the approximate length of time you will need to complete this task.

- Ways to monitor your physical and psychological welfare. Are you able to perform self-checks in both of these areas?
- How much time you can allot to complete this degree without losing too much time from your life/career? If you have taken time off previously in your doctoral journey, have you reviewed the possible impact it had on you at this stage in your career and as it relates to your family?

The reality of it all is that you may not have considered these questions and answers in great detail. You *have* been quite occupied! As you continue through the process, your focus may be getting through one class and/or project and then going on to the next. As you make your personal assessments to help prepare for the next phase, you will begin to have a lot of conversations with yourself. Honestly, that is not a bad thing. You may need to verbalize your areas of interest to gain a better understanding of how to approach these areas. As you review some of these areas, even more questions may need to be asked and answered. For example:

- Have I evaluated (recently) the amount of finances necessary to complete the degree?

- Have I looked into alternative ways to supplement the costs?
- How is my personal attitude about completing this task?
- Am I influenced or impacted by perceptions?
- Am I mindful of the impact that a reduction of time spent with those I am in a relationship with will have on me and them?
- Am I willing to spend an appropriate amount of quality time on completing this process and project?

I know that I have just thrown a lot of information at you, but the goal is to get you to consider *all* aspects of your decision to continue. At times you just look at the results without considering of all of the moving components that are necessary to continue to move forward to produce excellence in your performance. Honestly, on occasion you may not be aware of all that is necessary to complete the required tasks. However, not considering all of the areas that will be affected along the way often leads to greater difficulty in completing the task with excellent results.

Chapter 4

# Are You Serious? (The Reality Check)

## Phases and Levels of Seriousness

Seriousness, persistence, and earnestness are all characteristics needed to complete the doctoral program.

Although when you started this journey you knew you needed a certain level of dedication, you may not have understood the degree of the commitment needed to be successful. In other words, what you may have originally thought you needed in terms of time and money commitments may have only been the tip of the iceberg. As time progressed and you completed more classes, you may have noticed that this journey involved more time and dedication than you originally imagined, yet you still continued. What is important now is that you are in a different place. You have a stronger desire to see this process completed. What changed for you? Most likely your perspective changed. You now view these circumstances from a different vantage point. Because the doctoral journey is comprised of different phases, your perspective is also likely to change as you go through each one.

Through the coursework stage, you developed relationships with your peers. You conferred about ideas and exchanged knowledge. You maintained the posture of a student as you learned from your professors. Your level of dedication became cemented with every research paper and discussion feedback. You continued to evolve. As time progressed, you started to get a better understanding of the doctoral program. With each course behind you, it brought you closer to your goal—the completion of your doctoral degree. Through the phases of residency and your studies, you convinced yourself that you did in fact make the right decision. You fulfilled the necessary scholastic requirements and felt like you were a part of the process. You met new people, formed relationships, and participated in professional networks, and many of your contacts will become your lifelong professional peers. As you contemplate and internalize all that has occurred you realize that you have achieved a significant milestone. You have come to grips with the seriousness that is involved to achieve your scholastic goal and the psychological bond has been reinforced.

Are You Serious?

## Now That I Know Where I Am

As you draw closer to the completion of your coursework, you may have mixed emotions. "Should I just stop here now?" this maybe a passing thought. At some point, you may convince yourself that the title "ABD" (all but dissertation) doesn't seem that bad. It's not that you don't want to achieve your PhD; you may have a touch of fear, fear of the unknown, that is. The reality is that you have never traveled this road before. You don't know what to expect, so fear tends to be the dominating factor. It is important to align your next moves strategically for optimum performance. It is critical to resist the temptation to dismiss opportunities just because they are unfamiliar to you. Once you come to the realization that these experiences are to be expected, your level of seriousness and dedication changes, and your earnestness to achieve the end result becomes your motivating force.

## Plan of Action

*"If you fail to plan, you plan to fail."* We have heard that statement, but in order to be successful, you must not only have an action plan but an implementation strategy as well. While it is important to dedicate a specific amount of time toward your course work, it is also important to have a dedicated

space and resources to get things done. Now more than ever, the alignment of your priorities is of major importance as you continue forward. Conducting a gap analysis to establish where you are now compared to your desired outcome will help determine a direct course of action. Sometimes, you have to conduct your actions "on purpose." For example, what do you consider successful in this arena? Starting a timeline to establish some tangible boundaries for the process will ultimately provide a guide for you to follow with accountability checks as a by-product.

Although you may not be sure of the specific requirements (established by your institution) it would be helpful to have a period of time established in which you can work toward the completion of your degree. Based on your current lifestyle and responsibilities, you may want to give this some additional thought. You cannot go wrong if you are "planning on purpose" to do things within a specified period of time.

## Follow-Up and Follow Through

Have you ever wondered why some individuals are successful at achieving their goals and others are not? For example, every January some individuals make promises to themselves and others that they will use their gym membership this year with the ultimate goal of losing weight. Unfortunately for most, the gym membership ID gets filed away in their wallet or purse until something reminds them that they have gym privileges. Well, following up and following through not only requires action, but a level of certainty. To successfully achieve your goals, you must possess a level of certainty that the goals can be achieved. Conversely, a lack of certainty is accompanied by feelings of doubt and a host of mixed emotions. If doubt exists in your mind, it can lead to half hearted efforts and actions that will inhibit your success. To overcome these feelings (and to differentiate procrastination from lack of action) your goals must be clearly established with markers and monitors along the way.

Here are four suggestions to successfully implement your plan of action:

- First, surround your thoughts with positive feelings of certainty. To achieve this level of certainty, you need to set your goals in a framework that will stretch you, but not break you. Setting goals that are impossible to achieve will only lead to disillusionment and defeat.
- Second, once you are in the research process, set a limited number of actionable goals. Although this may sound elementary, most

people have the habit of setting too many goals at one time and then not doing a good job at accomplishing any of them. Having a lot of goals may create the illusion that you will achieve more, but that is not the case. Instead, start with a more manageable and realistic number of goals, three for example. Then as you achieve each goal, replace it with another one. Not only will you be able to stay on top of your goals, but it will help prevent feeling overwhelmed which could lead to inaction.

- Third, remind yourself of your goals. This should be done on a daily basis. Write your goals and create tools to constantly remind you of them. Sticky notes, vision boards or electronic reminders like voicemail or calendar reminders are great ways to keep your goals in front of you. Pick a method based on what is the easiest way to get your attention and use it consistently. Reinforcement with positive images and reminders will help keep you moving forward!

Now that you have established your goals and reminders getting into the habit of planning your day will help support the process even more. Not only will that be helpful in your research findings, but this effort will complement your writing as well. Taking this a step further, if you can establish a certain time of day to work on your project, it will lead to even more consistency in the process. The combination of consistent and constant action will result in increased momentum in your efforts. And, as a result, you will achieve your goals even faster.

- Lastly, participate in or host a support group. Remember, those who are striving for the same goals will not only understand your passion, but they will serve as a support system for you and vice-versa.

With the establishment of clarity of your goals, you will develop the art of follow through. This will allow you to enjoy the benefits of increased motivation, and excitement as your research comes to life through your documented findings.

The Dissertation Process

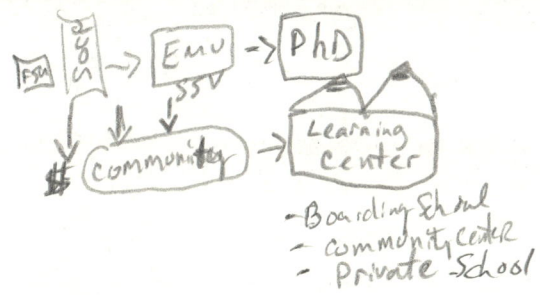

# Chapter 5
# I Can Research, I Can Write — Can't I? (Doubt)

## Second Guessing Yourself

Doubt or uncertainty, we all experience it at times. Now that you have completed several milestones in your doctoral journey, you can look back and see the choices that got you to this point. For example, the decision to attend college to pursue this advanced degree, completing the required coursework, along with passing the established criteria for advancement. As a result of achieving these various stages, you are now at the final stages of this program, and questions of uncertainty still arise and serve to keep you at a mental crossroad.

You may be thinking that it is strange to be experiencing this level of doubt now when you have come so far, yet it is still in the background causing you to second- guess your judgment. So from this point on, it is critical to make confident decisions that will lead to positive attitudes so you can turn your doubts into certainty. Here are five strategies to help you fend off doubts and stay on track as you continue to move forward.

1. **Measure your doubt against your values.** To get through this phase of doubt, you will have to answer some key questions. Does this project and the decisions I am making around it fit with my values? In the past, it was easier to see the link between your previous actions and their connection to your current status. You may have also made the decision to be a researcher or not to be one. However, in order to proceed now, it is important to review and align your choices with your values. Start by asking questions like, "Which decisions create an atmosphere of doubt?" Or, "Which thoughts are most reflective of the things that mean the most to me?" As long as they align with your core values, you will be okay, but if they don't your feelings of doubt may be trying to tell you something.

2. **Trust Your Gut and/or Instinct.** This is the point where you actually listen to your intuition. You should make it a point to dispel the "what ifs" and the inaccuracy of tiny details. It is also important that you move within the positive attitude that has brought you this far. You may ask questions such as: "Have you

achieved your prior goals?" "Was it difficult?" Sure, there were challenges, but you "knew" that you would get through that phase. Using hindsight, the challenges were not necessarily easy, but they weren't impossible either, and you were successful.

3. **It Just Doesn't Matter.** Sometimes you just have to pick your battles. This means making a continuous assessment of what is really important. And let me say at the onset, everything is not. Before plummeting yourself into doubt, evaluate your level of motivation along with your level of influence over a situation to determine possible outcomes. If it is worth fighting for, go for it. But if is not, let it go. Bombarding yourself with feelings of doubt does not equip you to be on the road to success. However, from time to time, you may need to ask yourself some pertinent questions to stay focused.

4. **Have enough information.** Before you start discounting your current situation, get as many facts as you can. This will allow you to make complex decisions when necessary. Writing a research paper or working on your dissertation is no easy feat. It is not only important, but imperative that you weigh all of the variables; the pros as well as the cons. From a realistic perspective, there is a

tremendous difference between just making a choice, and making a truly informed decision. In the process of your decision making, you will gain knowledge and information that will position you to become as prepared as possible.

5. **Respect your doubts. No one wants to be wrong.** We all shy away from change at one time or another because we are afraid of making a mistake. As a result of the possibility, staying where we are is always inviting because it is comfortable. This behavior can be defined as our "Gremlin." As Kevin Cashman states in his book, *The Leader from the Inside Out*, when becoming a leader, our Gremlins want us to avoid making mistakes at all costs. Although doubts exist, your Gremlin's role is to keep your doubts in check. There is a difference between valid doubts and managed doubts. Your Gremlin help you differentiate between what is relevant and what is irrelevant. It's like having "leadership" from the inside out. This concept is also present in a quote from James Freeman Clarke:

*"All the strength and force of man comes from his faith in things unseen. He who believes is strong; he who doubts is weak. Strong convictions precede great actions."*

To be successful on this doctoral journey, you have to take control of your doubts. And the solution could be as simple as a change in perspective.

*"Face your fear and doubts, and new worlds will open to you."* — Robert Kiyoski

## Where did you Get that idea?

Throughout your doctoral journey, you may have thought of possible research topics. While you may have vacillated between a good topic, a so-so topic, and one that was of great personal interest, you realized that at some point you would have to start narrowing your ideas. You may have asked your friends and colleagues their "opinion" of your research ideas. Then you were left to make the decision. With great trepidation you presented your research thoughts. You knew it could go either way. If it was well received with positive feedback, you could be free to mentally own the idea or topic at least partially. If on the other hand, it was not received favorably, you may have been tempted to disown the thought of pursuing this research idea further. Nonetheless, as time progresses, you will have to take possession of a topic. The question is "Where did you get that idea?" Chances are, your idea was influenced on several different levels. Knowing that ultimately this research is to contribute to a body of knowledge, you must establish that it is worth the exploration. You continue to gain extreme levels of confidence that this research can possibly be life-changing. Theoretically, you must stand behind your idea, and be prepared to defend your research topic and findings. You must always be strong in your convictions.

## How Do I Select a Topic?

The possibilities are endless. However, your choice of topics should be something that genuinely interests you. After all, you will be married to this idea for a significant period of time. Once you have an idea for a topic in mind, gather information on it. Specifically look for new findings that could make a significant contribution or an area of development that could be expanded. Ultimately, your research will brand you as an expert in your chosen subject matter, so you should have not only a current but an ongoing interest in it.

## Skill Set, Skill Level

In order for you to become a scholar practitioner, it is important to understand your existing skill set and level. Be as accurate as possible so that you set the correct expectations. For example, if you are highly gifted/talented in an area, make that clear. Beware of understating your skill set and level, such as describing yourself as a person who likes to draw while you possess the talents of Michelangelo. In fact, misinterpretations like this could raise questions about your ability; because of the way in which it was presented.

It is of the utmost importance that you assess your skill set by defining single units of competency for a specific need. Skill sets can be viewed as specific qualifications that are enhanced by various ranges of training. While going through this process and completing your project, it is important that a proper skill set is established, developed and nurtured. There are some questions that you will need to ask yourself: Do you have the ability to research this topic thoroughly? Or can you use creative alternatives that make use of your unique skill level? As time progresses, you should be able to provide specific answers to these questions.

## Accepting the Challenge of Being Challenged

Authority. Leadership. Brilliance. Integrity. These words independently speak volumes, and are audibly resounding when placed together. While in this research process, the characteristics of each of these words can and will echo independently. You may think that these words represent characteristics of individuals who sit on your committee very well. The reality is that those on your committee are not only equipped to be there, but they have a vested effort represented by their time to see you succeed. Because of their status as well as life experience, they will present constant and continuous challenges to you about your research.

It is important to mention that you should not take the comments made to you by your committee members personally. At this stage of the educational journey, it is imperative that you understand that the spirit of "excellence" is a key component. Work that is submitted should be of superior quality, and you should continuously strive for that.

From another perspective, most who are seeking to complete this degree have the characteristics of a leader. They have proven themselves in their community and in some cases exceptional professionally as well. Theoretically, leaders do not take instruction well or at all; but in this case, you must set that aside because accepting instruction is essential to being successful.

It is of great importance that you understand that while you are in this process of documenting your research project, you will not be in a leadership position. Because of your status in this equation, a different perspective is now warranted. Getting into the mode of not being in control can be a very unnerving thought; especially for those who have been in leadership roles prior. The fact is that even as a leader you must be accountable to someone. In this case, you are accountable for your actions to your superior, who is your Doctoral Chair. Overall, it is important that your skill and research not only co-exist, but compliment the project overall.

As you continue in this process, it is best to develop a positive attitude about being questioned. In conjunction with a positive attitude, it is also important to keep your "eyes on the prize." This will serve as a continuous, yet realistic reminder of the goal you are working toward.

# The Dissertation Process

## Chapter 6
# I'm Half-Way Through (Anticipation)

*Anticipation* is defined by Webster's dictionary as a prior action that takes into account or forestalls a later action.

Anticipation is one of those words that can go either way. It can create a smile or produce anxiety. Although it is defined with behavior that is contingent on something prior, it really comes down to a full level of expectation. I believe that we have varied degrees of anticipation that comes in specific stages of our lives. Since childhood we have expressed our defined levels of anticipation. We waited in anticipation for everything from birthdays, to holidays, to special events, to the arrival of family and friends. Then while attending school, we anticipated finishing our present course and the arrival of the next semester. Well, this mode doesn't stop. Anticipation continues to go with the flow of our lives. In this case, you have dedicated a significant period of time to your coursework. You have turned in project after project, paper after paper, with the expectation of receiving a grade. And now you are anticipating that all of your hard work will produce the desired degree.

The doctoral journey encompasses various phases. Each phase is contingent upon the completion of the last. As you travel through this process, you must not only realize the relevance of each phase but the importance of completing each one accurately as they build on each other. As a result, remember to develop patience while you are in the research process. It just makes the end result so much nicer.

## Confronting or Conforming — Which Is It?

Now that you have chosen your research topic and investigated it to some degree, you now have a certain level of confidence that grows as you learn even more. As time progresses, you will interact and have encounters with your committee members, especially your chair. Your conversations will be enlightening as well as challenging. At times you will question your position on your subject and your research. Based on the possible experience of your mentor, you may feel as if you are being attacked. In essence, you are being confronted. From your perspective, you will want to stand strong on your findings as you defend the relevance of your research.

## I'm Half-Way Through

But these actions can be tiring. So what's the best way to handle it?

First, take a few steps back. This will give you breathing room to assess the situation. Review all of the information that you have presented to your committee. Next, make notes on the comments that you have received. It is important that you access this information and then let it settle. Although it may be in your nature to make corrections immediately, it is best to revisit the research and comments in a day or so. With the passage of time, a new perspective may surface. Should you consider this a defeat? No. What you have done is revisited your findings from a different perspective. Please keep in mind this is still your idea. Take into consideration the context in which statements were made to you, in addition to the total perspective of your research. This review is not an abandonment of your ideas or thoughts, but a blended perspective (yours and others) of those who see this subject differently. At this point, some questions posed to you from those on your committee will help you establish greater clarity. The focus is and will remain that you develop a better understanding about your research and topic.

## Loving My Work

You have been working on this project for a significant amount of time. You have been challenged by your research committee members, along with their various opinions and views. The question is, "Are you still passionate about this subject?" Hopefully, you are. As previously mentioned, it is important that you love and understand why you have chosen this particular subject. Your position should be to learn as much as you can about your subject and field in general, so that you are knowledgeable about it on many different levels. As a personal challenge, you should find innovative ways to research your subject. Entertaining ideas such as attending seminars and reviewing books are just a couple of the ways you can stimulate your interests. It is also critical that you develop a working relationship with and about your research findings. Just as you would anticipate seeing a friend, you should view your research with eagerness and anticipation. Your attitude and approach will make a difference as you continue on this journey.

## Ways of Improving Because of New Findings

Although you are familiar with your subject matter, there are always new perspectives to be discovered.

Sometimes you find new information, and at other times, it may come from a committee member. Instead of just dismissing the information, first review it to determine its relevance to your subject matter. If a committee member has taken the time to research your subject, you should take his or her efforts seriously. Make an appointment to discuss their perspective regarding what was found and how he or she believes it fits with the focus you are pursuing. As you discuss their findings, also consider how this new information could be included to compliment your existing research work. Although your psychological perspective is one of anticipation, this action will set the tone for the next phase of making a determination of what to include and what to exclude.

## Inclusion vs. Exclusion

When we think of the words *inclusion and exclusion*, we tend to define them as opposites. Actually, they are not. The opposite of inclusion is not exclusion — it is not being included. There is a big difference. For example, if this research information is not included in the current work, it was not excluded; it was just not included.

Time has passed, and you have researched, written, interviewed, and tested your work. Now it is your turn to decide what is to be included and what is to be left out. You may ask yourself, "Can I really use all of this information?" Although you may want to use it all because it references your subject matter, that may not be feasible or your best option. You may want your research to have substance. Although all of the material may reference your subject matter, it is not all good; nor is it all relevant. Now you must determine what is pertinent and complimentary to your research.

Throughout my process, I learned this nugget of information from my doctoral chair, Dr. Michael McGivern. He said that there will be occasions where you will have to ask yourself these questions: "Is this information a *need to know* or is it a *nice to know*?" You will learn how to determine the relevance of what you should include as you continue on your journey. Your perspective of this (however) can lead you to a new attitude and viewpoint not only in your research, but you may find relevance in your life as well.

Chapter 7
# The Detours (Psychological Challenges)

## Life Happens

As you travel through the doctoral process, life has not stopped for you or those in and around your life. People continue to be born and die daily. Although it would be a wonderful thought to live in a concealed and excluded world as you go through the doctoral journey, the reality is that it does not happen that way. Your attachment to your work in the doctoral process must co-exist with the rest your life.

Just as one experiences various developmental phases of growth from infancy to adulthood, and because you are in this process for such an extensive period of time, you will go through several phases and challenges. During this time major life and lifestyle changes (both good and bad) may occur. The reason I mention this here is so that you will have a realistic view of the challenges that can occur outside the realm of your project. This is not to scare you but to inform you. As always, you will still need to address the challenge(s) and then return focused to your project. It is not only a project but a process.

## React or Respond

Because of your dedication to your work, you may appear fanatical to your family and friends. They may even label you with names that are (at times) offensive or demeaning. What do you do? Do you react or respond? Honestly, *this is an inevitable phase.* Those who are close to you probably have never witnessed this degree of dedication by you to a single process or project. This is can become much more time-consuming than "they" anticipated or allotted. Since they are not the focus (as they may have been in the past), they are faced with the reality that you are dedicating an exorbitant amount of time on something (other than them), and they can't quite understand. The reality is that they "will not" understand. The various phases that you have experienced and survived has not only enlightened you, but has equipped you for your continued journey. If you choose to react, it will be purely an act of aggression. If you respond, you should take your time to choose words that are clear and not ones that will hurt others. Remember, they are the ones reacting and it is your choice to react or respond.

## You Have Choices — Do You Make One?

As you continue, you may evaluate all that you have been through thus far. In your assessment, you may look at your accomplishments as minimal compared to the time you have invested. The reality is that we tend to judge ourselves harshly. You must learn to be fair, as people tend to criticize themselves with no mercy. Choices exist now as they have in the past, and, the question may present itself yet again, "Do you continue on the path or do you take the *all but dissertation* (ABD) road?" Yes, you have been challenged by your committee about your work. Yes, you have been challenged about your position and dedication to your family along with your level of personal and professional commitment. So what do you do now? Surprisingly, this question will surface again at this particular time because of the amount of pressure that you are now feeling. A good portion of that is because of the level of expectation and goals that you have established for yourself. The reality is if you want to continue, you will have to ask yourself again, "How badly do you want to complete this project in order to receive this degree?" You *must* be truthful to yourself. Ultimately, your answer will either provide fuel to continue or extinguish your desire. Think about it. Whatever your decision, make sure it is just that, your decision. Exclude all outside, influential factors that may have a bearing and make a decision based on your true inner feelings.

## Re-evaluating Everything — Sticking to Your Decision

This is one of the hardest phases that you will go through. You will come out of this with an incredible amount of maturity because of your truthfulness to yourself and to others as well. Yes, standing up for yourself is never easy, nor is it an action that you want to take on very often. However, now that you have done it, it is important to recognize that you are sticking to your decision. It is important from this time forward that you develop an attitude of a "DIT" (doctor in training) as you continue throughout the remainder of this journey. The reality of it all is that you are in the process of achieving the highest level of education, one that is only achieved by an elite few. You have now accepted the challenge 100 percent and all that comes with it. It is not always going to be an easy journey, but you are more than halfway there. Congratulate yourself and do something special for yourself today. You truly deserve it.

## Chapter 8

## Getting on Course Again (Educational and Self-Assessment)

### The Epiphany

As you survive the different psychological challenges that come with this process, you may have an epiphany. You no longer view the past with regret, but instead you anticipate a brighter future. Are things perfect? Of course not, but your perspective has shifted. How you approach your work (your attitude) will make a tremendous difference in the final work you produce. The "light bulb" has been turned on, and your illumination will be visible to all. Your attitude is contagious, and that is a wonderful position to be in!

### Re-evaluating How to Regain Lost Time

During the various challenges you have endured, you may feel that a significant amount of time was lost. Whether it equates to a week or six months; it is important that you re-evaluate and strategize your next steps. Although time has been spent, your perspective should be that it was necessary. And by no means was it lost. You came out from this experience with some valid "takeaways." You now have a better understanding of who you are as an individual, a scholar practitioner, a professional, and a family member. Your perspective is not only vital, but key here. Embrace this new understanding of yourself. You are this "total person" — a wonderful individual.

## Making Comparisons to Other Similarities in Your Life

You have lived a few years and have been through some stuff, yet you are still doing well. Some of the experiences that you have had during the doctoral process can be equated to things that you have already been through. How ironic is that? Many of the various phases that you have encountered while on this journey have an uncanny resemblance to phases of your life that you have experienced before. The wonderful thing about this discovery is that you can review and take note of the similarities. Ultimately, your story (if you decide to share it) will not only enlighten your journey, but help others gain a better perspective of life along with the highlights of this journey.

## Coming Back With a Vengeance

Looking back over the various stages that you have been through since committing to the doctoral process, you now realize that there have been several phases of development. At times, the momentum was energizing, while at other times it was minimal. You are now focused on completion of this degree and its achievement is starting to become more of a reality. The reality of you becoming a "doctor" is starting to take shape in your mind. Although you are still plagued with questions and doubts at times, you want to do well and make a significant mark on society. Dedication is now paramount for optimum performance. A tremendous amount of sacrifice is necessary to stay focused to continue and complete the journey. Once you have mentally and emotionally committed to its completion, your attitude will be strong with desire. Coming back with a vengeance to do this project will not only have a new meaning, you will be more passionate than ever before.

# The Dissertation Process

Chapter 9

# Smoother Sailing (Confidence)

*Confidence.* It can be described as a state of being certain that a prediction or hypothesis is correct and the best course of action. At times, we tend to lose our self-confidence. We second guess ourselves and our abilities. However, in reality things are becoming smoother with each passing day. You have developed a relationship with those who serve on your dissertation committee, and your conversations and interactions are not as strained as they were in the past. All in all, things are getting better.

This phase is more like being a participant in a choreographed exercise. You write and then submit your information. Next, you wait while your chair and committee review your proposal and dissertation draft. How long? On an average, you should expect that it may take up to two weeks to receive a response. Although you present your work with the expectation that it will be returned with few, if any negative comments, the reality of it being returned with significant comments always exist. So you wait with anticipation. Reflection is important here. How does that make you feel?

Remember that you, along with your dissertation committee chair and members, are responsible for creating a quality dissertation—one that could make a significant contribution to a body of knowledge. In order for this process to flow smoothly, keep in mind the specific roles of those involved. The role of the Doctoral Chair is to take primary responsibility for assisting you in the process. Your committee members are there to provide additional support and assistance as needed. Although your relationships are getting better, it is still ultimately your responsibility to produce quality work.

## Some Not Always Approved

Handling rejection is not easy, and it can be especially disheartening at this phase of the project. This is definitely one of those times where you may not be sure how to react. What is important here is that you realize that your main goal is to create the best possible research project and that is not any easy task.

Normally, the proposal and dissertation will require

multiple drafts, so prepare yourself for the return of your work, not once, but possibly several times. Your work will be reviewed on a regular basis, and it may not always meet the required standards. You may question yourself at times, but please be assured you will be fine. This is a part of the process that those who have completed it do not often mention, however it is a phase that everyone goes through.

## Re-evaluating the Subject Matter

Although you have written a lot on this research topic, there are still areas where it can be expanded or improved. Stop and ask yourself some pertinent questions like the following:

1. Have I expounded on the areas that would bring knowledge along with clarity to the reader?
2. Have I investigated this topic thoroughly?
3. Is my topic of interest?
4. Is my topic interesting in its *current* form?
5. What additional criteria and/or suggestions can I implement and include that will make this research engaging?

Once you receive comments from your committee, it is important that you process and evaluate the information you received. Here are some important steps to take in reviewing the comments you received in conjunction with your current material:

a. *Isolate the subject matter.* Now that you have received the latest version from your committee, review their comments. Look at this research exclusively by the subject matter and the context in which it was written and researched.

b. *Collect the statistics.* Does your research reflect the information that you are trying to convey correctly? Are there some gaps in the correlation of the statistics and the explained data?

c. *Take notes, evaluate, and read.* As you review the information your committee has provided, evaluate their comments. Read over your work with an objective mind. Make notes based on new findings and perspectives and incorporate their suggestions where appropriate.

d. *Think about your next move with this project.* Brainstorm your thoughts. Write down the immediate thoughts that come to mind. This will create an environment for the fostering of ideas. Mind mapping is a great tool to use here because it provides you with a pictorial

## Smoother Sailing

way of transferring ideas from your consciousness onto paper.

e. *Recall your thesis.* Don't lose the essence of your research. Always check to see if any new information or proposed changes will support your thesis? It is sometimes easy to wander off the path, but it is important that you remain focused as you go back and forth with your committee.

f. *Check your references.* Make sure that you have given credit to all of the information that you have cited. After a number of changes, it is easy to forget who said what. At times, you may have used a reference more than once. Review all your notes, and as you connect the references cited to your reference list, check them off. Double check each one to be sure they match.

g. *Re-examine your work.* Your work will be reviewed by your committee members as a scholarly submission. Your work must be that of a doctoral professional. It is of the utmost importance that you are clear and error free. Review and revise until you are sure, and consult an editor if necessary at this point.

## The Back and Forth Dance

During this stage, a dance appears to be going on. You submit your work and it is returned to you with comments and critiques. You make the revisions with caution and anticipation, hoping that this will be indeed your last waltz. Although it is possible that your work will be accepted, there is also the possibility that it will not be. Please do not get discouraged at this time, nor take these comments personally. It is of the upmost importance that you realize that you and your research are a "work in progress" so that you earn the title of "doctor" through your diligence. It is important that you stay focused and continue to develop your best researched work to date. Equate this dance to a competition where only those who remain are rewarded.

## Chapter 10

## Is the End Really in Sight? (Expectation)

Expectation refers to the act or state of anticipation. At this point you are anxious. You know that there is an end to this process, but you are not exactly sure when. With all of the edits from your committee, you may start to second guess your submission, your work, and the timeframe that you anticipated, along with a host of other important factors.

### Formulating Plans for Life After the Process

You are at the end of a process that had numerous steps. Are you happy to be here? Of course you are, although you are not sure how to express it. As time progresses you start to think about your current profession and the relevance of obtaining your degree.

So what's next? What did you learn through this process? How can you improve on you? As a "doctor," you will be expected to make a contribution to the body of knowledge. Your ideas will be welcomed as well as your innovative and creative perspectives. These are now some of the thoughts that you should entertain on a consistent basis.

## Getting Involved With Outside Professional Sources and Resources

As a scholar-practitioner, you may be required or expected to participate in professional organizations. There are hundreds of organizations in existence and a significant number are tailored to your area of expertise. Not only do these organizations present exclusive opportunities, they also represent a core group of individuals who have a common thread or theme. As you investigate these organizations, look at the benefits to being involved as well. I would encourage you to get involved on a local level first, and then upgrade to a regional status. As time progresses, you will be noticed for your consistent attendance. While getting acclimated, build a base of individuals who will hold you accountable.

Here are some strategies to help you get started:
1. Determine your primary objective for participating in professional organizations
2. Business connections
3. Volunteer opportunities

Chapter 11

# This Process CAN Become a Reality (Achievement)

You've been working on this project for quite some time now. At times it seemed endless, and your overall sentiments have always been that you just wanted it to be completed. However, beyond just completing the research portion of the project, you must also be prepared to defend what you have researched and written. This is where the "scholar-practitioner" designation comes into play and receives one of its biggest tests.

You are now approaching what I call the gray area of your journey—a rite of passage phase—and it is filled with uncertainty. However, having an intimate knowledge of your subject matter along with any specific additional requirements will enable you to approach it with increased confidence as you prepare and organize your defense.

## The Defense

*What exactly is it?* In essence, the defense is your opportunity to not only "defend" your work but to establish it as a needed contribution to the "body of knowledge." In order for your defense to be successful, you must be prepared. You have diligently researched and uncovered pertinent areas of your subject matter, including nuances that were thought to be non-existent. Now it is time to make the transition from your present stage to the fulfillment of what you have worked so long to accomplish — the title of doctor.

First, you must understand and become familiar with the established rules and protocol of your institution. For example, are the oral defenses done in a particular way? Are they held on a specific day or time? In some cases, specific departments allocate times for the oral defense to be completed. In general, the oral defense includes specific times for a presentation and a question and answered period. Each of these components is critical and essential. Although times differ from institution to institution, on an average, most defenses last approximately two hours, so it would be wise to be mentally prepared for at least that amount of time.

As you review existing protocols, you may also want

## The Process CAN Become a Reality

to meet with your committee chair to discuss anticipated work and an approach for your defense. Depending on the requirements, you may be asked to make a PowerPoint presentation as well. The goal of this presentation should be to summarize your research study and focus in on its most notable findings, so you will want to be selective in what you present. A couple of significant questions to ask to help you gain a better understanding of what to include are the following:

1. What do I want people to know about my dissertation?
2. What is the most important information that I can present and talk about to make my case?

By asking yourself these questions, you will be able to create a goal-oriented presentation that will enable you to guide your committee (or attendees) through a sequence of information that builds a clear defense with a focused direction. During this time, it's not unusual to ask yourself, "Who am I in this process?" This is a sign that you have matured and evolved into another phase—you are now a scholar-practitioner.

While in the preparation stages for your oral defense, you should have a clear understanding of who you are in this equation. The reality is that you should consider yourself as the authority of the information that is being presented. You are now in the position to be able to "instruct" your committee members as well as additional attendees. You should consider yourself an expert who has the ability to enlighten your audience about your research findings. As with any presentation, the organization of your material is a critical component to your success. Keep in mind that the essence of your PowerPoint slides is to present a summary of your dissertation research. The information presented should correlate with your research findings and clearly demonstrate the integrity of your work. However, remember no matter how elaborate your presentation is, do not fall into to the trap of interpreting it as the focus of your dissertation defense—your research and findings are still the focus.

## The Necessary Details

In preparation of your presentation, some specific areas should be addressed. Some common slides/areas include the following:

- Title of dissertation, including the presenter's name, department and date.
- Department dean (representative) and/or program of study.

- Committee acknowledgment
  While addressing the area of committee acknowledgment, be sure to include the names of the dissertation advisors and committee members. If time (and slide count) permits, you can also speak briefly about the contributions of each person to the success of your work. This may also be an opportunity to describe how you chose your particular research topic and the catalyst that led to your decision. In general, attendees are naturally curious about how researchers arrive at their research topics.

- Statement of problem
  Include a brief statement that outlines the particular circumstances of the research. In your role as the researcher, you can incorporate slides that statistically support data and information about the problem as well as components of the literature review for additional support. The goal here is to establish that this subject matter has earned merit based on the research you conducted.

- Significance of the research
  This is where you discuss the importance of your research and how it will impact the community at large. Be sure to include a list of all

of the research questions exactly as they appear in your written dissertation.

- Literature review
  This should include an overview perspective of your research, including the justification for your research advances and objectives.

- Method
  This should include an overview of the application methods used. Discuss specifically how your research was conducted along with critical information that highlights the reliability and validity of your research topic.

- Results and analysis
  This is your opportunity to include visual aids such as graphs, tables and charts that highlight the critical elements of your research findings. You can also include your hypothesis here as well.

- Discussion
  This is where you discuss the findings and the relevance along with the applicability to your field of expertise.

- Limitations of the study
  This should include an analysis of your work.

Explore questions such as: "If I had to conduct this study again, what would I do differently?" And, "Would another approach result in a different outcome, and if so, why?"

- Recommendations for future study
  Discuss the possibilities for the continuation of your work. This question provides existing and future students with the opportunity to get involved in conversation, possible conversion and the forum to contribute to the existing research.

### Final Preparation

Once you have completed your presentation or slide presentation and you have all of the logistical information such as the date, length of time, and other requirements, it is important that you rehearse your oral defense. This will provide you with a professional edge through reinforcement. In addition, here are a few specifics to remember:

1. Provide a hard copy of your presentation to each committee member and attendee *before* the defense date. Send an electronic copy to members who will be attending remotely.
2. Organize your personal items the evening before your presentation. It is also wise to do a

dress rehearsal of the clothing you will wear, along with a run-through of the materials. As a rule, you should dress as if you were delivering a paper at a conference or going to a job interview.
3. Lastly, keep the end goal in mind because all this will be behind you in a relatively short period of time.

## Getting Approved After the Approval

Once you have completed the oral defense, you will get feedback from your committee. If you have passed and have been approved, you will be addressed as "DOCTOR" for the very first time! Not only will you feel fantastic and euphoric, you will be recharged with an enormous amount of energy to see you through the final stages of this process.

To complete the next part of this stage, you will need the services of a professional editor. Even though you have passed the oral defense, the dissertation process is NOT complete at this time. A professional editor will be familiar with the *form and style* of dissertations as well as the latest version of the APA guide for citations. Your paper will not only meet all of the required guidelines,but it will also be polished and ready for publication. This is not the time to go

## The Process CAN Become a Reality

to someone that you know who majored in English in college. This document will be, in some cases, your first published work, and it needs to reflect scholarly content as well as excellence. Depending on the length of your dissertation and the amount of work that has to be reviewed, expect to pay $600 to $1200 in editorial costs.

However, before leaving this topic, I would be remiss if I did not discuss what happens in the unlikely event that you do not pass your defense. Let's look at a possible scenario. Honestly, this is highly unlikely, as you will be well prepared. Dependent on the guidelines of *your institution*, you may have an opportunity to redo your oral defense. At that point, the authorities of your university will be able to further instruct you on the progressive steps that must be taken and strictly adhered to. With that said, let's look at the pro-active measures that must be considered.

Prior to your defense, you will be well versed in your subject matter as an expert. Remember, you are the knowledge expert as you participate in your defense. Knowing all there is to know on the subject, in preparation of the defense process, you should make a list of anticipated questions that could be asked. The "what ifs" are the questions that you should consider, as well as the significance of your research. One typical question is, "How do you intend to make a contribution to the body of knowledge?" If you are able to answer this along with similar questions, you will be well prepared for your defense. Preparation is crucial as you head toward this final phase.

### Gearing Up for the Ceremony/Celebration

Before you know it, you will be tying up loose ends to complete your doctoral program. This is the time to ask questions about activities that are relevant to the completion of the program. Be sure to double check with your doctoral advisor to verify that you have successfully completed all of your academic requirements as well as your application for graduation.

Although this is a major step and an accomplishment, there are some that have no interest in attending the official ceremony. Whether you decide to attend or not, it is important to gather as much information as you can about the process, including any fees associated with graduation. Make sure that all fees are paid by the appointed date so that your name is visible on all printed graduation materials. And finally, don't forget to enjoy this exciting time. Your accomplishments are huge and well worth celebrating.

Chapter 12

# Closing Out This and Other Chapters in Your Life (Re-evaluation)

## Taking a Bird's-Eye View of This Process

A lot has been accomplished over your dissertation period. You have decided on a topic of interest, gathered information, and written and conferred with academic authorities. In addition, you have gained insights and grown your knowledge base about your subject matter. You have developed strong relationships with your committee members as you discussed various perspectives of your research. Some of your conversations were informative and enlightening, and some were disappointing. Nonetheless, you agreed with your academic mentors on your goal which was completing this process successfully and becoming a "doctor." Overall, this process has not only been a journey, but also a tremendously enlightening experience. It is now your responsibility to share your research findings with others and add to the body of knowledge.

## Reuniting with Family and Loved Ones

Although your family has been present, they have been in the distance. From your perspective, in order for you to get through the different stages of this process, there were times in which your contact with others was limited. This included events that occurred on a social level where you had to decline the invitation. At times, many did not understand your level of dedication to this process and project, but, you felt that you had no choice—you were on a mission. Now it is time to reconnect with family and friends. As you reach out into the social realm it is important to gradually immerse yourself in activities. You now have more time to participate in your social networks again, and it would appear that you will have to learn time management skills from another vantage point. Don't worry. This is all good. You haven't lost time; you have just allocated it in a different way for a relatively brief period of time.

## Assessing Relationships

Something major happens to our perspective when we go through a key transition in our lives. The completion of a doctoral degree is a tremendous feat. It not only requires discipline on the part of the participant, but it also requires a tremendous amount of

## Closing Out This and Other Chapters in Your Life

dedication on the part of the doctoral committee and chair. During this process, a new relationship is formed with its own dynamic. As you review your professional and academic relationships, your personal ones become more apparent. Based on your developed research skills, you may want to analyze everything, including almost everyone around you. At times, you will view those around you as simplistic; and in some cases, label them as "ignorant" because they are unfamiliar with your subject matter. Don't get caught up in the spirit of "elitism." It will not serve you well. The reality of it all is that you have *changed*. Your outlook and vantage point have been influenced and changed due to your total immersion in the dissertation process.

It is now your responsibility to make an effort to reestablish and, in some cases, mend relationships that have been compromised. From the perspective of your family members, their attitude is that they desire the best for you as you go forward. Unfortunately, they never anticipated the level of sacrifice necessary to achieve this goal. With that said, hopefully you can be empathetic to their feelings.

## Understanding Values: Mentally, Socially, Psychologically and Spiritually

Values are the cornerstone of development. They are different from attitudes and beliefs. Unlike attitudes and beliefs, values do need an object to focus on. Values work as the principle that allows you to give specific meaning to your experiences. They provide the ability to categorize and place each experience in some kind of systematic order, and they serve as a catalyst to produce your natural order of experiences as you categorize them by levels of importance, interest, relevance, and worth.

From time to time, re-evaluate our perception of ourselves and where we are in reference to the world. According to Socrates, you should "know thyself" (Socrates 470−399 BC). It is a part of human nature that after a major life-changing event, we tend to perform this evaluation as a self-check. In essence, all that we do and every perception that we have of the world around us is formulated over a period of time. These perceptions allow us to identify our "self." This can be classified as "emotional competency." This classification can also be reflected as a cycle as well: first, we have a view of ourselves; next, we are influenced by our perceptions; based on this our actions change not only the scenario and the world that we are involved in, but we are also

Closing Out This and Other Chapters in Your Life

Figure 3 Self-identification and emotional competency

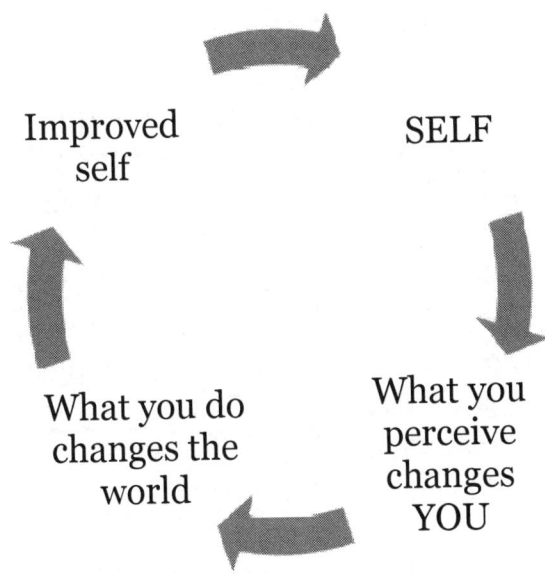

affected personally; lastly, we become an "improved self" version of ourselves. And the cycle of emotional competency repeats. See figure 3 above.

During this process, you become more aware of your values. As a result, a connection is made that forms links in your memory. For example, being praised for something and punished for something else leaves traces in our memory. If those traces are vivid enough, they can become powerful influences in your life. From a mental perspective, you will be tremendously influenced by the doctoral process for a significant period of your life, and you should not discount the impact of this life-changing event.

Socially, you have now become entrusted with a significant level of responsibility. As a result of your diligence and hard work, you have earned the title of "doctor." Not only are you now categorically in another place, your level of responsibility has increased. You now have a responsibility to contribute to the body of knowledge. (There is a reason I continuously mention this...) You represent not only yourself, but others who have gone before you in the quest for knowledge. As long as you have a working framework in which you are comfortable, you will perform well. According to Maslow's hierarchy of needs, the level referred to as *esteem needs* incorporates not only your self-esteem needs, but the esteem of others. In essence, once a person has satisfied his or her basic needs, the levels of concerns about worthiness emerge. Survival is no longer the focal point, but doing well (when judged by communal standards) is of great importance.

From a psychological perspective, values can be thought of as priorities and, in some cases, internal compasses or springboards for action. At times, we tend to use our concept of values as a general script in which we frame what is sought after, along with what should be avoided. Sometimes, when you analyze your values, you may ask the questions like, "Have my values changed as a result of my studies or research, and if so, to what degree?" You may further question: "Is this a change for the better?" Your answers to these questions can lead to further insights into your behavior and feelings about the doctoral process and your resulting dissertation.

From a spiritual perspective, you may have conferred with your source or a "higher power," especially in times of stress or need. You may have made promises and even made "deals" if they could only get you past some challenging points. Now that you have achieved your desire, it is time to acknowledge the source that you called upon because you did not do this alone. Re-establishing your spiritual relationship is also a good thing to do now.

# The Dissertation Process

Chapter 13

# True Self-Assessment (Reality)

## Understanding the Magnitude

Now that you have accomplished this major undertaking, it may at times be a lot to comprehend. Individuals will not only address you with your new title, they will have somewhat of an understanding of your accomplishments. Achieving a doctoral degree is not for the faint of heart. This task requires not only dedication, but determination as well. According to Phdcourse.net, although there is a desire to complete this degree when started, only 57 percent of students who begin a doctoral program complete their degree within a ten-year period. Approximately 30 percent will drop out or be dismissed, and the remaining 13 percent will continue on past ten years. In 2008, it was reported that only 1 percent of the US population had obtained this degree. Those statistics provide an even better understanding of the magnitude of what you have achieved.

## Embracing the Process

Although so much has been achieved, it may be quite difficult to embrace the entire process that has occurred. You have achieved a major task, and you should be proud of your accomplishments. As you recall the various phases that you have endured and survived, you should have a tremendous sense of triumph. You deserve all the accolades that come your way. You have achieved the highest degree of formal education.

Chapter 14

# Loving Me and Proud of It (Professional Assessment)

## Re-evaluation of the Work Completed – Registering With the Authorities (Validation)

As you go through the various end stages of your program, you will be continuously assessing your work as it is reviewed by numerous sources before your dissertation publication date. While protocols may vary from institution to institution, generally your work will be reviewed by your committee, your department chair, along with the dean of your professional college/ your scholastic discipline. Upon their approval, you will be *cleared* by the Institutional Review Board (IRB) for submission. (See the bonus chapter on the IRB for more information about the IRB process.) After you complete each of these stages, your work will be ready for submission to the UMI, who are the authorities for publication. Once your work is complete and ready for submission, it will be submitted to UMI/ProQuest. This organization has stringent rules and regulations for submission.

To reiterate this point, Roosevelt University (the Office of Graduate Studies & Research) has made available the necessary criteria for theses, dissertations, and doctoral projects. Here is a brief overview of the basic requirements:

- Paper size to be 8 ½ x 11" inches
- Margins of 1" on top, bottom, and right side
- Double spacing throughout, including reference lists, except for block quotes, footnotes and endnotes
- Use of TrueType font size 10 or 12
- For theses and dissertations written in languages other than English, a full document translated into English is required

## Understanding the Total Me

As you approach and go through these final stages, you will start to re-evaluate your current status in relationship to your achievements. You have been a student for a significant period of time, and now you are moving into another phase. It is important that you realize that you have grown considerably since you registered for your first doctoral class. You have been through some significant challenges on so many levels both professionally and academically as well as socially. At times, it is difficult to understand that all of this is happening to "you." As you reflect on your various phases of development, it can and will serve as a catalyst for your future endeavors.

The Dissertation Process

Chapter 15

# Let Me Share What I Have Done! (Pride and Satisfaction)

As you look back, it is important to note that your accomplishments are not just for you, but are to be shared with many. Your research, original work, and contributions have allowed you to earn the title of doctor. You should be proud to enlighten all who will listen.

## My Contribution to the Body of Knowledge

Your research topic was of importance and of interest to you. Being a doctor, has allowed you to gather important information and findings that are current and relevant. Now that you are an authority on your subject matter, you have a responsibility to enlighten those who are interested. As time progresses, you will discover many venues and forums in which you can share your research. As a strategy, it is important to make a list of organizations and conferences along with symposiums where your information can gain additional exposure. Your level of contribution to the body of knowledge is up to you and your ability to enlighten all who are interested is endless.

## Plans from This Point On — Assessment On a Regular Basis

Have you considered which path you will travel with your research? Have you considered ways of sharing your knowledge? Are you interested in focusing on conducting further research on your topic? Are you planning on providing lecturers or informational sessions about your subject matter? Which way do you want to go? These are some thoughts that you need to consider in detail.

As you review your research, you will need to reassess its validity. You may find ways to improve upon your existing research, collaborate with another authority in your field, or add to your existing work. Whatever your decision, be prepared to do it with excellence. That level of quality is now expected of you.

## How Do I Keep the Passion Going?

Your subject matter was of interest when you made the selection to investigate it for additional information and research. You were (and still may be) excited about your subject and willing to explore different facets of it. If so, your passion could be ignited for years! On a regular basis, encourage friends and colleagues to discuss their interests. See if there is any correlation or if one can be developed between your subject matter and their interests. As time progresses, you may find ways to marry two researched ideas and develop a new research study and hypotheses. Always be on the lookout for opportunities to develop additional interest in your subject matter. As you continue on your quest, your passion will be never-ending. It is an inevitable part of the process.

## Giving Back

You have reached the end of your formal academic journey. Not only have you been successful, you have done well. As a doctor, you are expected to make contributions besides academically. You may ask yourself: "In what capacity can I do this?"

Earlier, we discussed possible ways of sharing your knowledge base. Although the prior ways mentioned are typical, you may have some additional creative ideas. What is important is that you share your knowledge. It may come in a form of volunteering, community service, or writing an article or a book. Don't limit yourself to the understanding that you have gained in this process; it is yours to share.

## Closing Thoughts

As we have taken this journey together, we have discovered different phases and challenges in the process. Yes, it is true; going through a doctoral program is no joke. In the past, it was difficult to determine what to expect from a psychological or mentored perspective as you went through the doctoral process and that is one of the main reasons for this book.

In the first few chapters, you had to come to grips with quite a few emotions. You had to recognize the magnitude of the commitment. Were you ready? Probably not, but you still had to prepare yourself as much as possible as for the life-changing questions that came your way. You assessed and you recognized that there were not only sacrifices to be made, but consequences related to your actions.

Doubt had you second guessing yourself and your ability. Are you smart enough? Are you worthy? These and other questions kept coming up as you continued the process. Finally, you made a conscious decision to persevere and be the best that you could possibly be. Through it all, you still had a high degree of anticipation. Just as a child gets excited about being in a candy store, you started to recognize the magnitude of the scholastic degree and, in part, the associated responsibility that came with what you were pursuing. Did you understand it fully? Of course not; however, you did understand it enough to keep the excitement and momentum going.

During the next phase, no one could have prepared you for the psychological challenges that you would encounter. At times, it probably seemed as though life had passed you by in the social realm. You were present, yet you missed much. The level of dedication needed was paramount in your mind as you focused on the prize. In the interim, family and friends felt like they were in a second place position to your emotions and commitments. Were you wrong for choosing to prioritize completing the program? No. A high level of commitment was mandatory. You recognized that you would be able to resume your life and lifestyle in the near future. The trade off (if there was one) was that the time spent with non-school related items would be limited.

There were times in the journey when you had to make an educational and self-assessment. Although many of the scenarios presented themselves at the most inopportune time, you dealt with the unexpected. You recognized that change *can* be good.

## Closing Thought

As you focused on the research of your topic, you gained a sense of confidence. You developed confidence in what you were researching and the findings along with your own self-discoveries in the process. Were you out of the woods? No. You just developed a greater understanding as you reassessed and re-evaluated the information you collected. In route, you realized that this process had several facets. You learned that scholastic requirements and the formulation of your research was not only in a long-term relationship, but a possible marriage because commitment on both parts was essential.

You danced with the dissertation committee more frequently than you liked, but now in retrospect, you are enlightened with a better perspective of the timing that is needed for a wonderfully choreographed effort on both parts. You are now better.

Your level of expectation has also changed. You had to start thinking about your role after you completed this awesome process. How are you planning to make your contribution to the body of knowledge? What will *you* be known for? As you start to contemplate your areas of research, you get excited with your level of expectation. Although you are not sure of what to expect, you are pleased. Your vantage point has changed and you now look at the glimmering light that you have seen all along as "hope." That

## The Dissertation Process

thought alone has made your heart smile.

Have you considered all the phases of development in writing a dissertation? *Probably not.* You have been forced to assess your current life and lifestyle along with the impact of this project on every aspect of your life: mentally, socially, psychologically, and spiritually. As you take the time to apply your new level of improved performance, you are now better because of the experience. Your reality has allowed you to embrace the process and gain a better understanding of the magnitude along with a comfort level of who you have become. It was a challenge, but it is **done**.

You now know that you have developed into a "total individual." You are now been empowered with all the professional responsibilities that the title of doctor has to offer. Your unnoticed level of pride is well deserved. You have achieved an enormous task of which you should have an incredible amount of satisfaction.

My final words to you are that *I am proud of you and your achievements.* In order for you to do well in any aspect of your life, both the application of knowledge and the collection of information are critical. You represent a small part of the world's population to be awarded the title of doctor. I hope this book has

## Closing Thought

served you well as a guide, a mentor, and a voice of understanding as you worked toward this significant milestone in your life. And, now it is your obligation to share.

I wish you all the best that life has to offer in your new professional role.

Dr. Claudia

The Dissertation Process

# APPENDIX A:

## Understanding the Established Requirements

As you pass each milestone, new challenges appear. Is that a bad thing? No, it's just part of the process. As you are now aware, this process involves numerous steps. To give you an idea of what to expect, this bonus section includes two important components that don't always get a lot of attention: the order of things and the Institutional Review Board (IRB).

### Understanding the Order of Things

As you proceed mentally with the process of writing the dissertation, it would be helpful to gain an understanding of how a research project is developed and assembled. To give you an extra edge, I have outlined the "foundational" components of the dissertation below. I have not included the abstract, table of contents, table of figures or references that are standard components of research documents.

Components of the Dissertation
- Introduction
- Review of the Literature or Literature Review

- Methodology
- Results
- Conclusions

**Introduction**
In this section, you will identify your problem for your audience. You are wondering, "where do I find my problem"? Some possible sources include information or papers from a previous course, reviewed articles or a source that you intended to investigate further. *In actuality, this will probably be the most challenging part of your dissertation.* Your problem may start out very large or vague as your quest, (at least for now)is to change the world. However, as you will quickly learn, your problem must be manageable; given time and money constraints to research this area. It is important that the topic you select has a foundation. This means thatthere have been some previous studies or research in this area or related to your problem or research topic in some way. It is helpful if there is existing information upon which you can build your research. This information can be in the form of recent theoretical sources, tested surveys,observation instruments, or previous studies. This type of information will provide a wonderful base for your research so that once you have decided on a problem that you have the desire to work on,you will have the documentation to make this a valid

Appendix A

research subject. That leads us tothe next section that authenticates the history of the topic in existing literature.

**Review of the Literature or Literature Review**
Now that you have chosen an area of interest, please be assured that problems that are deemed interesting always have a history behind them that can be investigated; even if it is only a theoretical context presented in the past. Although there may not be an exact match in existing literature that has "your name on it" in terms of what you want to focus on, there is often a visible correlation between what you are interested in investigating and the history and context of current research. For example, you may start off with a topic of interest, but presently there may not be a published work on it. This then can be the focus of your study. Your literature review should thoroughly examine all of the available information in detail. Here you can describe the study that you propose to do and analyze where the existing information falls short. During this process, you will be describing your ideas along with the ideas of others to make sense of things, along with the exposure of what ideas are missing. As a result, the theoretical context of your study gets mapped out. In this section, it is important that you do not use this as an opportunity to make this an all-out Internet or library search of sources. It is a strategized "limited" section

of the best examples of the most recent writings about the problems you are working on. It is a critical analysis of the ideas that you will use to discuss your problem, along with the actual researched studies previously conducted upon which you can build your work. The wonderful aspect that must be considered is that you can also include information that omits or uncovers shortcomings that assist in justifying the need for your work to be performed and investigated further. This overall is a good thing.

## Methodology

This section provides a road map of what you have done. This includes a description of your methods of analysis, statistical techniques, and how you selected participants (subjects) for your research. To insure that you have covered the important aspects of this section, review the selection methods and techniques that you have chosen to use. Are they the best methods or techniques for the type of problem that you are studying? Is your description of the research able to be duplicated? In other words, could someone else continue this study if you were not able to? This area should be so clear that it could be reproduced, if necessary, with other participants to achieve similar, if not the exact same results. If this is true, you have done well in this area.

Appendix A

## Results

The formulation of this section is heavily dependent on the type of research that you have chosen. The interpretation of data and the direct correlation of what you have researched are identified here. This section tells all of what you have done. This explains your researched work, the passion of what you are doing, and the documentation that justifies your findings. Although this sounds easy and straightforward, it can be a bit of a challenge.

It is important, in this section, that you report the *facts* of your findings. When conducting a statistical analysis, it is important that you do not manipulate your data to achieve your desired findings. Focus on reporting only relevant data related to the questions asked. And, at this point, it's not unusual to begin second guessing yourself on the information cited. Have you reported enough? In this case, a summary will not be sufficient. This is where you will need to use and consult the professional judgment of your peers, colleagues, and committee members. Your doctoral chair should also be able to assist you in determining the level of reporting that is necessary. When in doubt, ask.

## Conclusion

This section can be a challenge. This is where you

evaluate your work – your research. A fundamental question that will be posed to you in this area is, *"So what now?"* Now that you have discovered and uncovered this vital information, what's the next move? To assist your audience in understanding this next move, you must explain the results of your research and their meaning. How important is your discovery? What is its relevance to your theory? Based on what you have discovered, is there a need or a reason for further research?

As you discuss the successes and failures of your findings, make a note of whether or not they yielded your expected results. If not, that should be a part of your findings, but *this does not mean that you have failed.* What it does reveal is that this area of research may need to be further investigated, possibly from a different perspective.

Psychologically, it was a discovery, but not a waste. Your findings may vary from your conclusions. You have negotiated the various levels of emotions and discovered a new unbiased aspect of your research. You can now speak with authority about your subject matter. You are a scholar-practitioner.

Now that you have an outline of what is expected, you are prepared for the progression of the project. Although this is great, this process does not exempt

## Appendix A

you from the psychological challenges that you will inevitably face. With each phase of development of your research and writing you will experience some hill and valley experiences from the actual work and emotional perspective. Because these challenges are anticipated, you will be able to recognize each phase as it occurs. The next sections provide an overview of some of the inevitable psychological phases.

*Personal Note: We have reviewed the requirements necessary to get us to the next level. By discussing what is anticipated you will have a better handle of what is expected. Conversely, from a psychological perspective, you will experience an array of emotions. Although you are outlined with the requirements from your institution to conduct an efficient research study, you were not informed about the emotional challenges. Is that a bad thing? No; not really. As in life, there will be consistent challenges that will occur on a regular basis. This experience is no exception to the rule. Through the various phases of this dissertation process, you will feel many ups and downs. Are they preventable? Probably not; but this insight will give you a better perspective of what is anticipated. Here are some of the phases that have been experienced by most on this journey.*

The Dissertation Process

# APPENDIX B:

## Preparing for the Institutional Review Board (IRB)

The Institutional Review Board (IRB) is a committee that monitors, reviews, and approves the behavioral and biomedical research that involves humans. It was established so that the welfare and rights of research participants' are monitored and always protected. So if your project will involve human subjects, this is one of the steps you will need to go through to get approval for your project. Some of the elements that need to be addressed prior to receiving approval to use human research subjects include specific information about your study and proposed subjects. This includes age, the nature of your study, questions to be asked, along with the environment in which your study will be conducted. Overall, your questions will have to be posed in such a way that no one involved will take offense.

The IRB has developed a detailed process that you will need to follow including a short course that will introduce you to the ethics of being involved in research along with its methods. The goal is to sensitize you regarding the use of research subjects and steps to protect their safety. As you get closer to this requirement, your institution and possibly your doctoral committee chair will be able to assist and inform you of the necessary tasks to be completed. Here is a brief overview of the necessary steps in completing an IRB review:

1. Complete the IRB application.

2. Present a detailed description of your research, including your hypotheses, methods or procedures to be used, along with a detailed description of the population that you will be studying. You will also be expected to describe the steps that you will take to minimize possible risks to the participants and to maintain their confidentiality.

3. If grants or other dissertation proposals are associated with your research, you will need to submit a copy of those documents.

4. Submit copies of any surveys, sample questions and/or questionnaires you will be using.

5. Submit copies of recruitment materials that you may use to enlist your subjects. This includes any contact letters, e-mails, phone scripts, and flyers.

6. Provide a detailed description of any secondary data you will use. This should also include the source, the variables that it contains and any merging you will do with

## Appendix B

other data sources as well as any agreements you that you have made with the owners of the data. Also, if your research will be conducted through the collaboration with another organization, you will need to document that the organization involved is in agreement with and approves your research. And, they may need IRB approval as well. This and similar requirements exist for those who are interested in conducting research overseas. It will be best to check to see if there is any existing policy with your institution concerning international research and if this applies to your research study.

7. Lastly, submit copies of consent forms, assent forms, and any translations that are applicable. Finally, don't forget, if your research involves the use of patients' medical records, you may be required to use a HIPPA authorization form or consent. You can check further into this information through your school to investigate any existing policies. A direct website link may exist that will possibly connect your access to HIPPA protocol.

As you can see, this phase can be quite involved and time-consuming. Unfortunately, this part of the dissertation process is often missing in discussions of what is needed, but it is a requirement for those of you who will be dealing with live subjects. In general, understanding the IRB process will give you an "edge" or an advantage that many others will not have.

Depending on the nature of your research, there will be times where you will be challenged by your subject matter. There will be emotional periods where you will question the nature and validity of your research study and the "whys" of performing one. Do not despair. This emotional reaction is the norm. You will achieve success as a result of knowing what to expect. Now that you have considered the ethics of involving participants in your study, you will become more mindful of other factors that will impact you greatly along the way. In the past we discussed the costs of this commitment on a semester-by-semester basis. Now, it is imperative that you consider these other areas as well, whether they are emotional, psychological, or ethical in nature.

# References

Cashman, K (2008). *Leadership from the Inside Out.* San Francisco, CA: Berrett-Koehler.

Deci, E.L. 1980. *The Psychology of Self-Determination.* Lexington, MA: D.C. Health (Lexington Books).

Maslow, Abraham H. 1968. *Toward Psychology of Being.* 2nd ed. New York: van Norstrand, Reinhold.

Maslow, A. 1954. *Motivation and Personality.* New York: Harper.

© Abraham Maslow original Hierarchy of Needs concept 1954; Alan Chapman review and other material design, code 1995–2010.www.businessballs.com
Peterson's Graduate Schools — http://www.petersons.com/graduate-schools/phd-programs-rigorous-educational.aspx

http://phdcourse.net/united-states/united-states.

Roosevelt University office of Graduate Studies www.roosevelt.edu/Provost/~media/Files/pdfss/Prvost/Graduate/UMI.ashx

Rubie-Davies, C. 2006 "Teacher Expectations and Student Self-Perceptions: Exploring Relationships," *43* (5), 537–552.

Trautwein, U., O. Ludtke, G. Nagy, and H.W. Marsh. 2009. "Within-School Social Comparisons: How Students Perceive the Standing of Their Class Predicts Academic Self-Concept." *Journal of Educational Psychology 101(4).* 853–866.

## About the Author

Dr. Claudia Barnett is a training and performance improvement technologist and a graduate professor. She holds a PhD in training and performance improvement, a master's degree in industrial organizational development and human behavior, and she is the CEO of CGB Associates, an Educational and Performance Improvement company. Dr. Barnett also teaches adult learners including physicians and nurses as well as business owners, and graduate students on a regular basis.

With over 27 years' experience in training, her real passion is to mentor those that she comes in contact with on a daily basis, and she has served as a doctoral mentor for numerous individuals who have successfully completed their PhD journey. She currently serves as the chair of the Volunteer Committee for the International Society for Performance Improvement (ISPI) and is an editorial contributor to their website. Dr. Barnett is a sought after speaker and lecturer.

To learn more, visit her website: www.thedissertationprocess.com or contact her directly at info@thedissertationprocess.com.

Made in the USA
Middletown, DE
17 June 2016